D0428111

KANA
CAN
BE EASY

絵で覚える
ひらがな・カタカナ

by Kunihiko Ogawa

The Japan Times

Originally published in 1975 as a service to the faculty
and students of San Diego State University.
Copyright © 1975 by Kunihiko Ogawa

Copyright © 1990 by Kunihiko Ogawa

All rights reserved. No part of this publication may be
reproduced in whole or in part, by photo copy, mimeograph,or any other means,
without the prior written permission of the publisher.

First edition: May 1990
36th printing: August 2010

Illustrations: Kumiko Ichikawa
Layout & Jacket design: CADEC, Inc.

Published by The Japan Times, Ltd.
5-4, Shibaura 4-chome, Minato-ku, Tokyo 108-0023, Japan
Phone: 03-3453-2013
http://bookclub.japantimes.co.jp/

ISBN4-7890-0517-8
Printed in Japan

PREFACE

It is well-known that the Japanese writing system, among those of the world languages, is uniquely complex. It involves *kanji* (Chinese characters), *hiragana* and *katakana* (the two types of the Japanese syllabaries), and *rōmaji* (the Roman alphabet). To those learning the language, this complex writing system is indeed a serious liability which cannot be avoided.

This book is intended to ease the burden for such learners by introducing the two types of the Japanese syllabaries, *hiragana* and *katakana*, through a method which is intended to assist in memorizing, recognizing and producing each *kana* (syllabary) through pictorial association. For example, the *hiragana* "*ku*" or く happens to be shaped like the widely opened bill of, say, a *cuckoo*; thus the shape and sound of the *hiragana* "*ku*" can be easily connected to each other through the picture of a cuckoo.

Early mastery of the *kana* is an unavoidable necessity. It is the author's sincere hope that this book will minimize the learners' time and mental fatigue in learning the *kana* and will rather make this learning experience, which is otherwise somewhat tedious, quick and fun.

This book is the completely modified version of my *Mnemonic Aids to the Japanese Syllabaries* which was published by San Diego State University in 1975. I am indebted to Conan Grames, with whom I taught Japanese at the University of Utah, for inspiring some of the original ideas.

Special thanks are due to Fujiko Motohashi for her many helpful comments and suggestions. Thanks also go to Jackie Rives for her sound advice. I am especially grateful to Chiaki Kaku for her inestimable assistance in the editing of this manuscript.

Kunihiko Ogawa
Kofu, Japan
May 1990

3

CONTENTS

HOW TO USE THIS BOOK

A.

1. On each page, the large picture in the upper right-hand corner ① is designed to help you associate the sound and shape of the Japanese syllabary systems (*kana*, or *hiragana* and *katakana*). Look at the picture, and read the caption ②, trying to associate the picture with the crucial sound indicated in boldface in the underlined word. The crucial sound in the caption is intended as a helpful approximation to the proper reading of each *kana*.

2. Spend a few minutes until you can visualize the picture and its accompanying caption in your head.

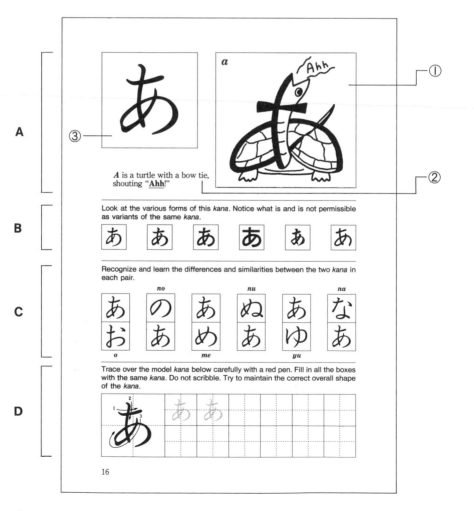

A is a turtle with a bow tie, shouting "**Ahh!**"

Look at the various forms of this *kana*. Notice what is and is not permissible as variants of the same *kana*.

Recognize and learn the differences and similarities between the two *kana* in each pair.

Trace over the model *kana* below carefully with a red pen. Fill in all the boxes with the same *kana*. Do not scribble. Try to maintain the correct overall shape of the *kana*.

16

3. Compare the picture with the corresponding *kana* to the left of it ③. Pay attention to every detail of the model *kana*.
4. Cover the *kana* with your hand, and look at the picture again. Do this until you can visualize the *kana* clearly in the picture.
5. Next, cover the picture with your hand, and keep looking at the *kana* until you can visualize the picture in the *kana*.
6. Now cover both the picture and the caption with your hand(s), and keep looking at the *kana* until you can visualize the picture and recall the crucial sound in the caption.

B. Next, look at the alternative examples of the *kana*. You may see these various forms in Japanese publications and writing.

C. Then look at the pairs of *kana* in the center of the page. Notice the differences and similarities between the *kana* in question and the other paired with it. Some differences which may look trivial to you are very significant in differentiating *kana*. On the other hand, there are some insignificant differences among variants of the same *kana* which may look important to you.

D. Now trace over the model *kana* in the first two boxes at the bottom of the page with a red pen or something which is not black color. Take care to maintain the correct overall shape. Fill in all the remaining boxes with the same *kana*. Make sure to center the *kana* in each box, not too big or not too small for the box. Write very deliberately; common mistakes are hurrying too much, drawing meaningless lines, omitting important lines, and curving, slanting, or straightening lines in the wrong manner. Never scribble.

●Repeat this process for each page.
●After every ten pages, test your memory of the *kana* you have learned.
●Before proceeding to the *katakana* section, review the total *hiragana* section completely. The thorough mastery of *hiragana* will make it easy to learn *katakana* because many *katakana* resemble corresponding *hiragana*.

INTRODUCTION

◉What is *kana*?

Until about the fifth century A.D., Japan had no writing system of her own. Then, the introduction of *kanji*, as Chinese characters are called in Japan, made it possible to write the Japanese language. Although Chinese characters had their own original particular Chinese sounds and meanings, they were mainly adapted to Japanese as *kanji* by selecting only those characters whose Chinese meanings matched or approximated those of the Japanese language.

Because there were many cases where Japanese grammar was different from Chinese so that no Chinese characters exactly corresponded to the meanings of Japanese (for example, particles, verb and adjective endings), some *kanji* were used merely as phonetic signs or syllabaries representing Japanese sounds without regard to their original Chinese meanings. The number of such *kanji* was gradually narrowed down to some fifty, the minimum number which can represent Japanese syllables. Eventually the Japanese syllabaries called *hiragana* and *katakana* replaced such *kanji*.

It is said that *hiragana* were originated by a woman or women in the early Heian period (therefore, once called *onna moji*, or women's characters) on the basis of modifying the shape of *kanji* so as to be written quickly in a cursive, flowing style without lifting the brush. *Katakana* were developed by many people including Buddhist monks also in the Heian period on the basis of adopting just one portion of *kanji*, rather than the entire shape. For example, see the following:

	KANJI	HIRAGANA	KATAKAKA
"na"	奈	な	ナ

The *hiragana* "na" is a simplified, modified form of the entire corresponding *kanji* "na", while the *katakana* "na" consists only of the upper left of the corresponding *kanji*.

Much later in the sixteenth century, European missionaries started to come to Japan. They introduced the Roman alphabet or *rōmaji* to Japan. Since then, Japanese can be represented entirely by *rōmaji* if necessary.

◉The current Japanese writing system

Japanese sentences can be written vertically, top to bottom, right to left. The front pages of newspapers and books published in Japanese start on the opposite side of those published in English. Some books and scientific papers and documents containing Arabic numerals, formulae and foreign words are usually written horizontally, left to right, like those published in English. There is no special spacing between words in a sentence unlike English, but punctuation

8

marks such as commas and periods (small circles in Japanese) are used in Japanese.

Kanji, *hiragana* and *katakana* are used in ordinary writing. Usually, though not strictly mandatorily, *kanji* are used for expressing "meaningful" elements such as nouns and stems of adjectives and verbs. *Hiragana* are used for expressing "grammatical" elements such as particles, and endings of adjectives and verbs which show tenses, etc. *Katakana* are usually reserved for "loan" words borrowed from Indo-European languages (e.g., "television", "radio"). In addition, *rōmaji* may also be used to write Japanese. Its use is generally confined to names of train stations, stores, companies, modern store merchandise and the like. This is often intended for the convenience of foreigners in Japan or as a kind of fashionable decoration.

It is possible to write an entire Japanese sentence in *hiragana*. If an adult forgets certain *kanji* which are rarely used, he may substitute *hiragana* for them. Since the basic 46 *hiragana* symbols and some modifications of them suffice for all Japanese sounds, Japanese children start to read and write Japanese all in *hiragana* before making an attempt to learn some two thousand *kanji* currently used.

●*Kana, rōmaji* and the Japanese syllables

If you agree that Spanish is an easy language to pronounce, you will also admit that Japanese pronunciation presents very few problems to most foreign students. Thus *rōmaji*, which are not rigid phonetic signs, can function as convenient representation of Japanese for those whose languages make use of the Roman alphabet.

Japanese has five vowels, thirteen consonants and two semi-vowels, all of which make up 104 syllables. Each combination stands for each syllable. It is these syllables that are represented by *hiragana* or *katakana* syllabaries. Forty-six basic *hiragana/katakana* represent 46 syllables, and all the remaining syllables can be represented by these *hiragana/katakana* with slight modifications. The syllables are presented by the following chart in the order given in Japanese schools.

There are two Romanization systems: the conventional Hepburn System still widely used, and the official *Kunreishiki* System ("Official System") designated for use in Japanese schools. Between the two, Hepburn presents closer approximations to "real" sounds than *Kunreishiki*, though *Kunreishiki* has more uniformity in representation than Hepburn.

RŌMAJI and *HIRAGANA*

〔*Rōmaji* in ( ) are written according to the *Kunreishiki* System.〕

Basic *hiragana*

a	あ	*i*	い	*u*	う	*e*	え	*o*	お
ka	か	*ki*	き	*ku*	く	*ke*	け	*ko*	こ
sa	さ	*shi* *(si)*	し	*su*	す	*se*	せ	*so*	そ
ta	た	*chi* *(ti)*	ち	*tsu* *(tu)*	つ	*te*	て	*to*	と
na	な	*ni*	に	*nu*	ぬ	*ne*	ね	*no*	の
ha	は	*hi*	ひ	*fu* *(hu)*	ふ	*he*	へ	*ho*	ほ
ma	ま	*mi*	み	*mu*	む	*me*	め	*mo*	も
ya	や			*yu*	ゆ			*yo*	よ
ra	ら	*ri*	り	*ru*	る	*re*	れ	*ro*	ろ
wa	わ							*o*	を
n	ん								

Hiragana with two dots/a little circle

ga が	*gi* ぎ	*gu* ぐ	*ge* げ	*go* ご
za ざ	*ji (zi)* じ	*zu* ず	*ze* ぜ	*zo* ぞ
da だ	*ji (zi)* ぢ	*zu* づ	*de* で	*do* ど
ba ば	*bi* び	*bu* ぶ	*be* べ	*bo* ぼ
pa ぱ	*pi* ぴ	*pu* ぷ	*pe* ぺ	*po* ぽ

Hiragana with small や (*ya*), ゆ (*yu*), よ (*yo*)

kya きゃ	*kyu* きゅ	*kyo* きょ
sha (sya) しゃ	*shu (syu)* しゅ	*sho (syo)* しょ
cha (tya) ちゃ	*chu (tyu)* ちゅ	*cho (tyo)* ちょ
nya にゃ	*nyu* にゅ	*nyo* にょ
hya ひゃ	*hyu* ひゅ	*hyo* ひょ
mya みゃ	*myu* みゅ	*myo* みょ
rya りゃ	*ryu* りゅ	*ryo* りょ
gya ぎゃ	*gyu* ぎゅ	*gyo* ぎょ
ja (zya) じゃ	*ju (zyu)* じゅ	*jo (zyo)* じょ
bya びゃ	*byu* びゅ	*byo* びょ
pya ぴゃ	*pyu* ぴゅ	*pyo* ぴょ

RŌMAJI and *KATAKANA*

〔*Rōmaji* in ( ) are written according to the *Kunreishiki* System.〕

Basic *katakana*

a	ア	*i*	イ	*u*	ウ	*e*	エ	*o*	オ
ka	カ	*ki*	キ	*ku*	ク	*ke*	ケ	*ko*	コ
sa	サ	*shi* (*si*)	シ	*su*	ス	*se*	セ	*so*	ソ
ta	タ	*chi* (*ti*)	チ	*tsu* (*tu*)	ツ	*te*	テ	*to*	ト
na	ナ	*ni*	ニ	*nu*	ヌ	*ne*	ネ	*no*	ノ
ha	ハ	*hi*	ヒ	*fu* (*hu*)	フ	*he*	ヘ	*ho*	ホ
ma	マ	*mi*	ミ	*mu*	ム	*me*	メ	*mo*	モ
ya	ヤ			*yu*	ユ			*yo*	ヨ
ra	ラ	*ri*	リ	*ru*	ル	*re*	レ	*ro*	ロ
wa	ワ							*o*	ヲ
n	ン								

Katakana with two dots/a little circle

ga	ガ	gi	ギ	gu	グ	ge	ゲ	go	ゴ
za	ザ	ji (zi)	ジ	zu	ズ	ze	ゼ	zo	ゾ
da	ダ	ji (zi)	ヂ	zu	ヅ	de	デ	do	ド
ba	バ	bi	ビ	bu	ブ	be	ベ	bo	ボ
pa	パ	pi	ピ	pu	プ	pe	ペ	po	ポ

Katakana with small ヤ (ya), ユ (yu), ヨ (yo)

kya	キャ	kyu	キュ	kyo	キョ
sha (sya)	シャ	shu (syu)	シュ	sho (syo)	ショ
cha (tya)	チャ	chu (tyu)	チュ	cho (tyo)	チョ
nya	ニャ	nyu	ニュ	nyo	ニョ
hya	ヒャ	hyu	ヒュ	hyo	ヒョ
mya	ミャ	myu	ミュ	myo	ミョ
rya	リャ	ryu	リュ	ryo	リョ
gya	ギャ	gyu	ギュ	gyo	ギョ
ja (zya)	ジャ	ju (zyu)	ジュ	jo (zyo)	ジョ
bya	ビャ	byu	ビュ	byo	ビョ
pya	ピャ	pyu	ピュ	pyo	ピョ

HIRAGANA

As shown by the chart below, there are 46 basic *hiragana* signs represent-ing 46 syllables. All the remaining syllables can be represented by these basic signs with slight modifications. Therefore, it is of great importance to master these 46 basic signs as early as possible in your study of Japanese. The modifications which are needed for the remaining syllables will be explained at the end of this book.

	a	i	u	e	o
	あ	い	う	え	お
k-	か	き	く	け	こ
s-	さ	し	す	せ	そ
t-	た	ち	つ	て	と
n-	な	に	ぬ	ね	の
h-	は	ひ	ふ	へ	ほ
m-	ま	み	む	め	も
y-	や		ゆ		よ
r-	ら	り	る	れ	ろ
w-	わ				を
n	ん				

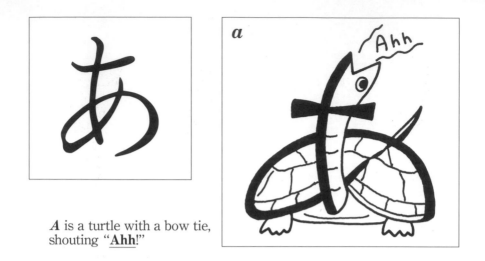

A is a turtle with a bow tie, shouting "**Ahh!**"

Look at the various forms of this *kana*. Notice what is and is not permissible as variants of the same *kana*.

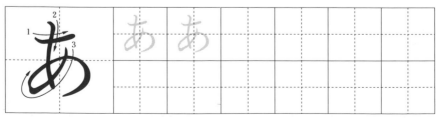

Recognize and learn the differences and similarities between the two *kana* in each pair.

Trace over the model *kana* below carefully with a red pen. Fill in all the boxes with the same *kana*. Do not scribble. Try to maintain the correct overall shape of the *kana*.

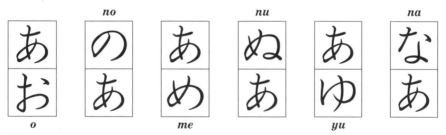

16

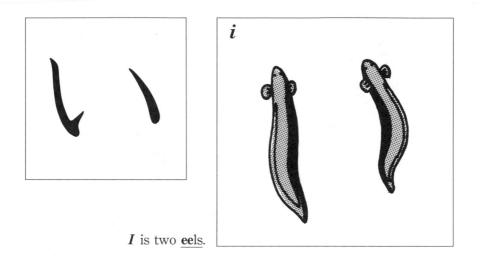

I is two **ee**ls.

Look at the various forms of this *kana*. Notice what is and is not permissible as variants of the same *kana*.

Recognize and learn the differences and similarities between the two *kana* in each pair.

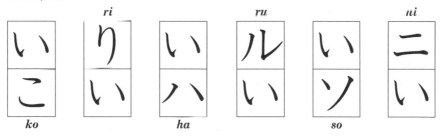

Trace over the model *kana* below carefully with a red pen. Fill in all the boxes with the same *kana*. Do not scribble. Try to maintain the correct overall shape of the *kana*.

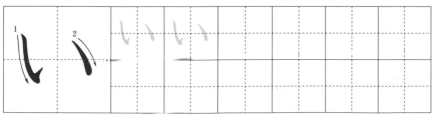

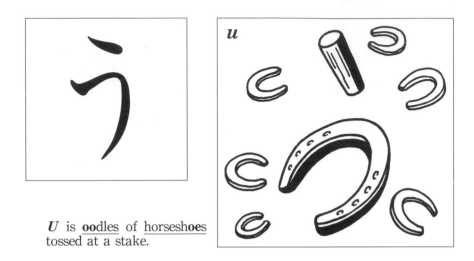

U is **oo**dles of horsesh**oe**s tossed at a stake.

Look at the various forms of this *kana*. Notice what is and is not permissible as variants of the same *kana*.

Recognize and learn the differences and similarities between the two *kana* in each pair.

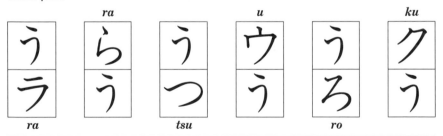

ra   **u**   **ku**

ra   tsu   ro

Trace over the model *kana* below carefully with a red pen. Fill in all the boxes with the same *kana*. Do not scribble. Try to maintain the correct overall shape of the *kana*.

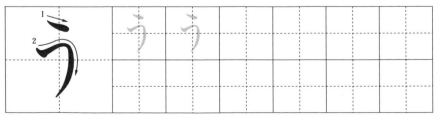

E is an <u>e</u>lf.

Look at the various forms of this *kana*. Notice what is and is not permissible as variants of the same *kana*.

Recognize and learn the differences and similarities between the two *kana* in each pair.

Trace over the model *kana* below carefully with a red pen. Fill in all the boxes with the same *kana*. Do not scribble. Try to maintain the correct overall shape of the *kana*.

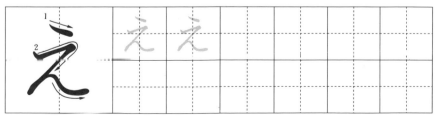

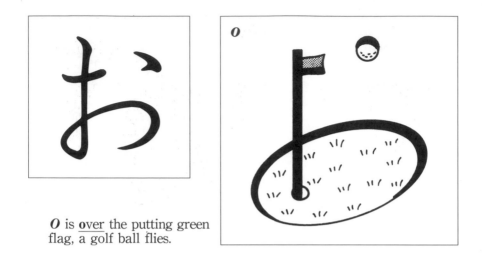

O is <u>o</u>ver the putting green flag, a golf ball flies.

Look at the various forms of this *kana*. Notice what is and is not permissible as variants of the same *kana*.

Recognize and learn the differences and similarities between the two *kana* in each pair.

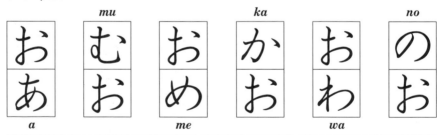

Trace over the model *kana* below carefully with a red pen. Fill in all the boxes with the same *kana*. Do not scribble. Try to maintain the correct overall shape of the *kana*.

ka

Kahh!

Ka is the "**Kahh**!" of a crow behind a bent old woman.

Look at the various forms of this *kana*. Notice what is and is not permissible as variants of the same *kana*.

Recognize and learn the differences and similarities between the two *kana* in each pair.

ke *u* *wa*

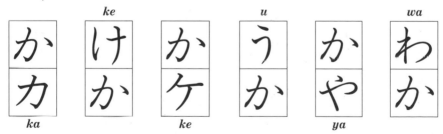

ka *ke* *ya*

Trace over the model *kana* below carefully with a red pen. Fill in all the boxes with the same *kana*. Do not scribble. Try to maintain the correct overall shape of the *kana*.

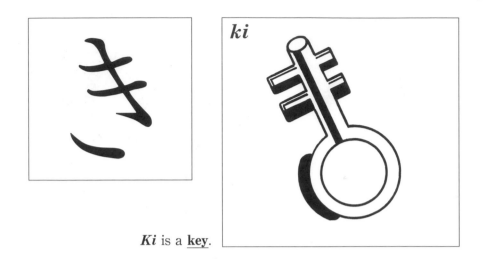

Ki is a <u>key</u>.

Look at the various forms of this *kana*. Notice what is and is not permissible as variants of the same *kana*.

Recognize and learn the differences and similarities between the two *kana* in each pair.

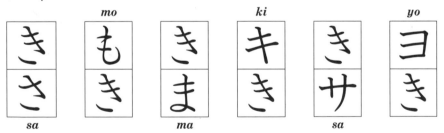

Trace over the model *kana* below carefully with a red pen. Fill in all the boxes with the same *kana*. Do not scribble. Try to maintain the correct overall shape of the *kana*.

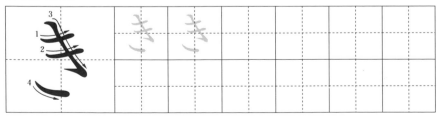

22

_Ku_ is a <u>cuckoo</u>'s bill.

Look at the various forms of this *kana*. Notice what is and is not permissible as variants of the same *kana*.

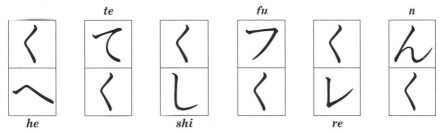

Recognize and learn the differences and similarities between the two *kana* in each pair.

te

fu

n

he

shi

re

Trace over the model *kana* below carefully with a red pen. Fill in all the boxes with the same *kana*. Do not scribble. Try to maintain the correct overall shape of the *kana*.

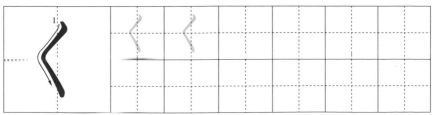

Ke is one boxer being <u>KO</u>'d by another.

Look at the various forms of this *kana*. Notice what is and is not permissible as variants of the same *kana*.

け	け	け	け	け	つ

Recognize and learn the differences and similarities between the two *kana* in each pair.

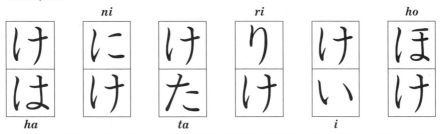

Trace over the model *kana* below carefully with a red pen. Fill in all the boxes with the same *kana*. Do not scribble. Try to maintain the correct overall shape of the *kana*.

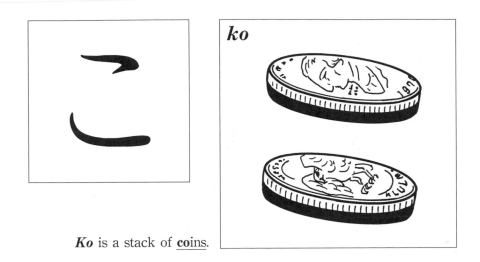

ko

Ko is a stack of **co**ins.

Look at the various forms of this *kana*. Notice what is and is not permissible as variants of the same *kana*.

Recognize and learn the differences and similarities between the two *kana* in each pair.

Trace over the model *kana* below carefully with a red pen. Fill in all the boxes with the same *kana*. Do not scribble. Try to maintain the correct overall shape of the *kana*.

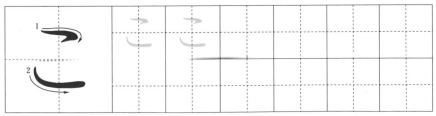

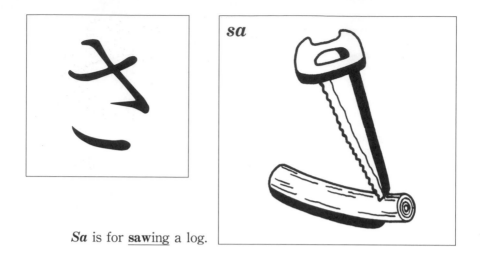

Sa is for **saw**ing a log.

Look at the various forms of this *kana*. Notice what is and is not permissible as variants of the same *kana*.

Recognize and learn the differences and similarities between the two *kana* in each pair.

Trace over the model *kana* below carefully with a red pen. Fill in all the boxes with the same *kana*. Do not scribble. Try to maintain the correct overall shape of the *kana*.

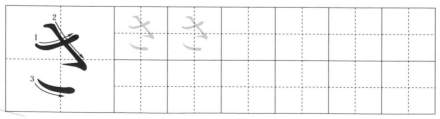

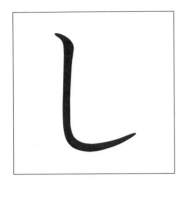

Shi is for "**She** has a pony-tail."

Look at the various forms of this *kana*. Notice what is and is not permissible as variants of the same *kana*.

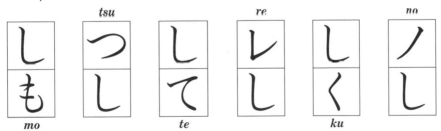

Recognize and learn the differences and similarities between the two *kana* in each pair.

 tsu *re* *no*

mo   *te*   *ku*

Trace over the model *kana* below carefully with a red pen. Fill in all the boxes with the same *kana*. Do not scribble. Try to maintain the correct overall shape of the *kana*.

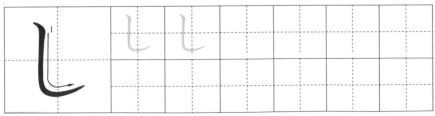

27

su

Su is "**Soo**ey, **soo**ey!" you call out to a pig with a curly tail.

Look at the various forms of this *kana*. Notice what is and is not permissible as variants of the same *kana*.

Recognize and learn the differences and similarities between the two *kana* in each pair.

Trace over the model *kana* below carefully with a red pen. Fill in all the boxes with the same *kana*. Do not scribble. Try to maintain the correct overall shape of the *kana*.

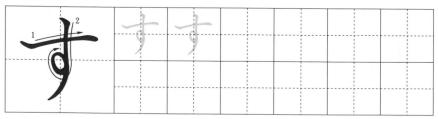

se

Se is to **say** "I love you!" on your boyfriend's lap.

Look at the various forms of this *kana*. Notice what is and is not permissible as variants of the same *kana*.

せ	せ	せ	せ	せ	せ

Recognize and learn the differences and similarities between the two *kana* in each pair.

mi

ya

se

ke

ya

se

sa

Trace over the model *kana* below carefully with a red pen. Fill in all the boxes with the same *kana*. Do not scribble. Try to maintain the correct overall shape of the *kana*.

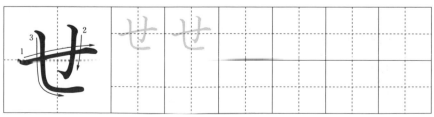

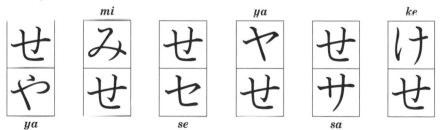

29

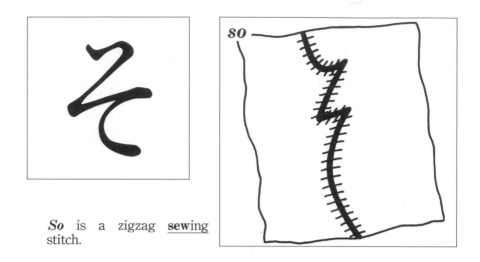

So is a zigzag **sew**ing stitch.

Look at the various forms of this *kana*. Notice what is and is not permissible as variants of the same *kana*.

Recognize and learn the differences and similarities between the two *kana* in each pair.

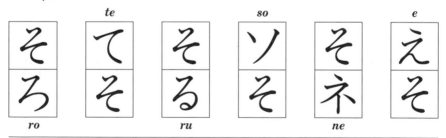

Trace over the model *kana* below carefully with a red pen. Fill in all the boxes with the same *kana*. Do not scribble. Try to maintain the correct overall shape of the *kana*.

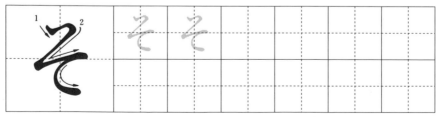

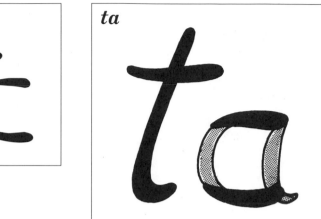

ta

Ta is like the letters "**ta**."

Look at the various forms of this *kana*. Notice what is and is not permissible as variants of the same *kana*.

た　た　た　た　た　た

Recognize and learn the differences and similarities between the two *kana* in each pair.

 ha **ke** **o**

ni　　　*na*　　　*ho*

Trace over the model *kana* below carefully with a red pen. Fill in all the boxes with the same *kana*. Do not scribble. Try to maintain the correct overall shape of the *kana*.

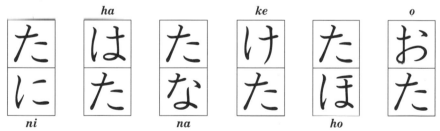

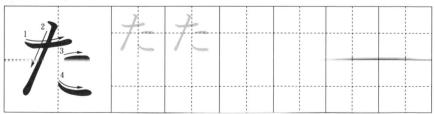

Chi is a **chee**rleader.

Look at the various forms of this *kana*. Notice what is and is not permissible as variants of the same *kana*.

Recognize and learn the differences and similarities between the two *kana* in each pair.

Trace over the model *kana* below carefully with a red pen. Fill in all the boxes with the same *kana*. Do not scribble. Try to maintain the correct overall shape of the *kana*.

tsu

Tsu is a <u>tsu</u>nami, a huge sea wave.

Look at the various forms of this *kana*. Notice what is and is not permissible as variants of the same *kana*.

Recognize and learn the differences and similarities between the two *kana* in each pair.

	te		*he*		*ra*
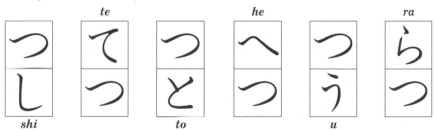
shi		*to*		*u*	

Trace over the model *kana* below carefully with a red pen. Fill in all the boxes with the same *kana*. Do not scribble. Try to maintain the correct overall shape of the *kana*.

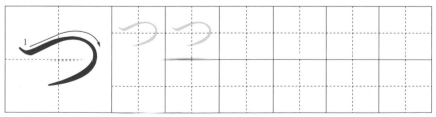

33

te

Te is the __tail__ of a dog.

Look at the various forms of this *kana*. Notice what is and is not permissible as variants of the same *kana*.

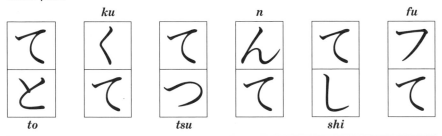

Recognize and learn the differences and similarities between the two *kana* in each pair.

ku

n

fu

to　　　　*tsu*　　　　*shi*

Trace over the model *kana* below carefully with a red pen. Fill in all the boxes with the same *kana*. Do not scribble. Try to maintain the correct overall shape of the *kana*.

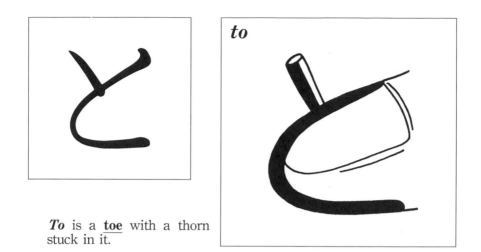

to

To is a **toe** with a thorn stuck in it.

Look at the various forms of this *kana*. Notice what is and is not permissible as variants of the same *kana*.

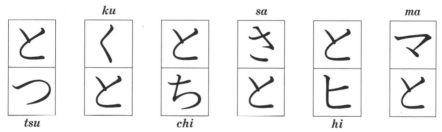

Recognize and learn the differences and similarities between the two *kana* in each pair.

 ku

 sa

 ma

tsu *chi* *hi*

Trace over the model *kana* below carefully with a red pen. Fill in all the boxes with the same *kana*. Do not scribble. Try to maintain the correct overall shape of the *kana*.

Na is someone **kno**cking at the door.

Look at the various forms of this *kana*. Notice what is and is not permissible as variants of the same *kana*.

Recognize and learn the differences and similarities between the two *kana* in each pair.

	ta		*ho*		*mu*

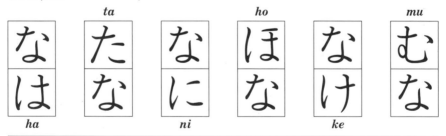

ha   *ni*   *ke*

Trace over the model *kana* below carefully with a red pen. Fill in all the boxes with the same *kana*. Do not scribble. Try to maintain the correct overall shape of the *kana*.

36

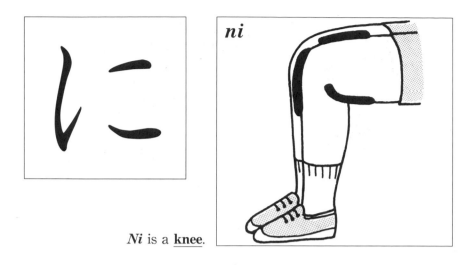

Ni is a **knee**.

Look at the various forms of this *kana*. Notice what is and is not permissible as variants of the same *kana*.

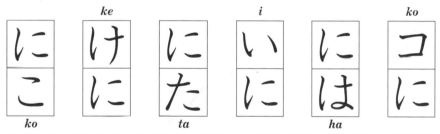

Recognize and learn the differences and similarities between the two *kana* in each pair.

ke

i

ko

ko ta ha

Trace over the model *kana* below carefully with a red pen. Fill in all the boxes with the same *kana*. Do not scribble. Try to maintain the correct overall shape of the *kana*.

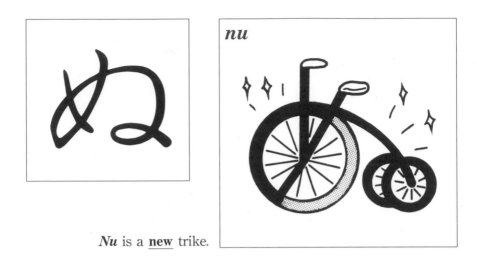

nu

Nu is a **new** trike.

Look at the various forms of this *kana*. Notice what is and is not permissible as variants of the same *kana*.

Recognize and learn the differences and similarities between the two *kana* in each pair.

ne   *a*   *o*

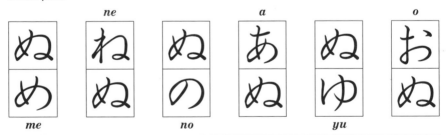

me   *no*   *yu*

Trace over the model *kana* below carefully with a red pen. Fill in all the boxes with the same *kana*. Do not scribble. Try to maintain the correct overall shape of the *kana*.

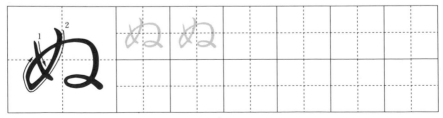

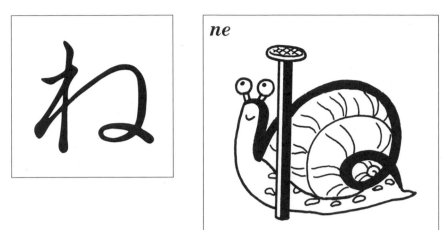

ne

Ne is a <u>snai</u>l behind a <u>nai</u>l.

Look at the various forms of this *kana*. Notice what is and is not permissible as variants of the same *kana*.

Recognize and learn the differences and similarities between the two *kana* in each pair.

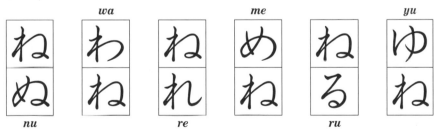

wa *me* *yu*

nu *re* *ru*

Trace over the model *kana* below carefully with a red pen. Fill in all the boxes with the same *kana*. Do not scribble. Try to maintain the correct overall shape of the *kana*.

no

No is a **no** entry sign.

Look at the various forms of this *kana*. Notice what is and is not permissible as variants of the same *kana*.

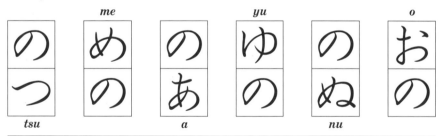

Recognize and learn the differences and similarities between the two *kana* in each pair.

tsu

 me

 yu

a

 o

nu

Trace over the model *kana* below carefully with a red pen. Fill in all the boxes with the same *kana*. Do not scribble. Try to maintain the correct overall shape of the *kana*.

ha

Ha is a <u>ho</u>ckey player sitting on a bench.

Look at the various forms of this *kana*. Notice what is and is not permissible as variants of the same *kana*.

Recognize and learn the differences and similarities between the two *kana* in each pair.

	ni		*ke*		*ta*
は	に	は	け	は	た
ほ	は	ま	は	な	は
ho		*ma*		*na*	

Trace over the model *kana* below carefully with a red pen. Fill in all the boxes with the same *kana*. Do not scribble. Try to maintain the correct overall shape of the *kana*.

_Hi_ is to laugh "**Hee-hee**!"

Look at the various forms of this *kana*. Notice what is and is not permissible as variants of the same *kana*.

Recognize and learn the differences and similarities between the two *kana* in each pair.

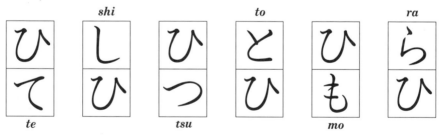

Trace over the model *kana* below carefully with a red pen. Fill in all the boxes with the same *kana*. Do not scribble. Try to maintain the correct overall shape of the *kana*.

42

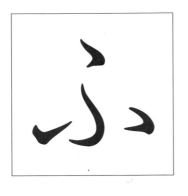

fu/hu

Fu/Hu is Mt. **Fu**ji with a
path down the middle.

Look at the various forms of this *kana*. Notice what is and is not permissible
as variants of the same *kana*.

Recognize and learn the differences and similarities between the two *kana* in
each pair.

Trace over the model *kana* below carefully with a red pen. Fill in all the boxes
with the same *kana*. Do not scribble. Try to maintain the correct overall shape
of the *kana*.

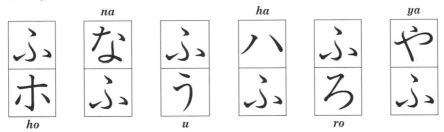

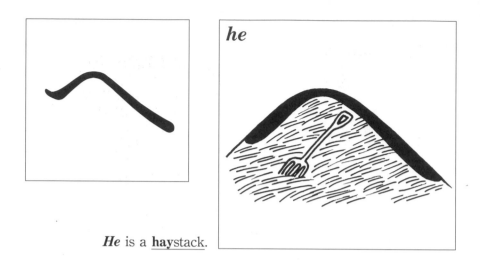

He is a **hay**stack.

Look at the various forms of this *kana*. Notice what is and is not permissible as variants of the same *kana*.

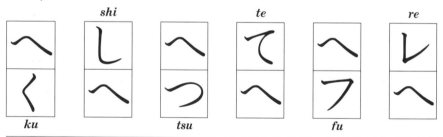

Recognize and learn the differences and similarities between the two *kana* in each pair.

 shi *te* *re*

ku   *tsu*   *fu*

Trace over the model *kana* below carefully with a red pen. Fill in all the boxes with the same *kana*. Do not scribble. Try to maintain the correct overall shape of the *kana*.

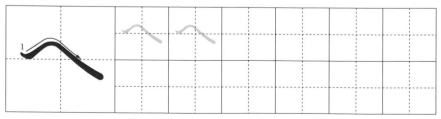

ho

Ho is a **hoe** held by a farmer with a big hat, sitting with his legs crossed.

Look at the various forms of this *kana*. Notice what is and is not permissible as variants of the same *kana*.

ほ ほ ほ ほ ほ ほ

Recognize and learn the differences and similarities between the two *kana* in each pair.

 ke   *ni* *ki*

ha   *ma*   *na*

Trace over the model *kana* below carefully with a red pen. Fill in all the boxes with the same *kana*. Do not scribble. Try to maintain the correct overall shape of the *kana*.

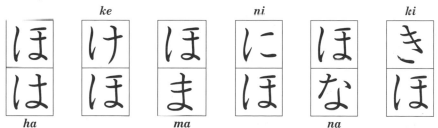

ma

Ma is Grand**ma** with a hat.

Look at the various forms of this *kana*. Notice what is and is not permissible as variants of the same *kana*.

Recognize and learn the differences and similarities between the two *kana* in each pair.

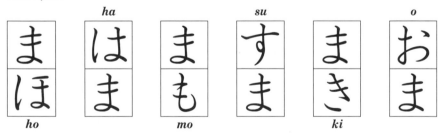

Trace over the model *kana* below carefully with a red pen. Fill in all the boxes with the same *kana*. Do not scribble. Try to maintain the correct overall shape of the *kana*.

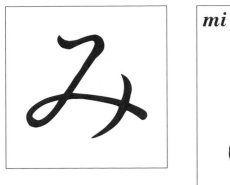

Mi is **me**, 21 years old, a nice age to be.

Look at the various forms of this *kana*. Notice what is and is not permissible as variants of the same *kana*.

み　み　み　み　み　み

Recognize and learn the differences and similarities between the two *kana* in each pair.

　 se / me　 ro / mu　 ma / mi

ya　me　mu

Trace over the model *kana* below carefully with a red pen. Fill in all the boxes with the same *kana*. Do not scribble. Try to maintain the correct overall shape of the *kana*.

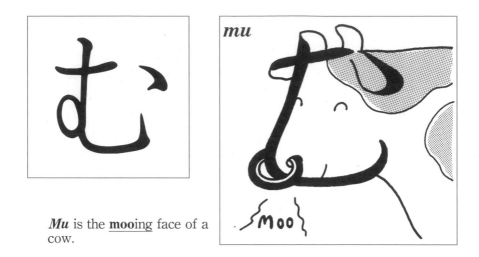

mu

Mu is the **moo**ing face of a cow.

Look at the various forms of this *kana*. Notice what is and is not permissible as variants of the same *kana*.

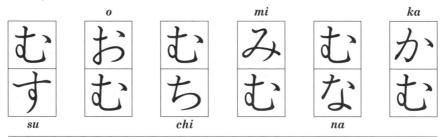

Recognize and learn the differences and similarities between the two *kana* in each pair.

  o *mi* *ka*

su   *chi*   *na*

Trace over the model *kana* below carefully with a red pen. Fill in all the boxes with the same *kana*. Do not scribble. Try to maintain the correct overall shape of the *kana*.

me

Me is the **ma**ne of a horse.

Look at the various forms of this *kana*. Notice what is and is not permissible as variants of the same *kana*.

Recognize and learn the differences and similarities between the two *kana* in each pair.

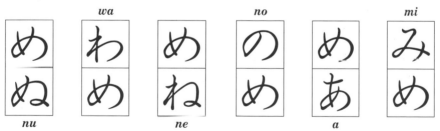

wa   *no*   *mi*

nu   *ne*   *a*

Trace over the model *kana* below carefully with a red pen. Fill in all the boxes with the same *kana*. Do not scribble. Try to maintain the correct overall shape of the *kana*.

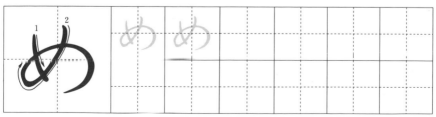

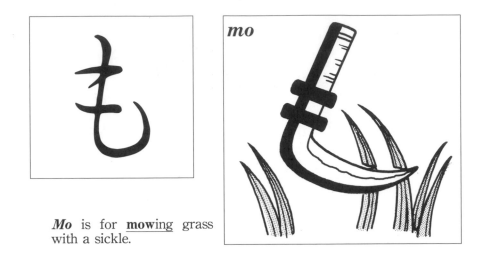

mo

Mo is for **mo**wing grass with a sickle.

Look at the various forms of this *kana*. Notice what is and is not permissible as variants of the same *kana*.

Recognize and learn the differences and similarities between the two *kana* in each pair.

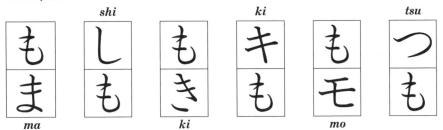

Trace over the model *kana* below carefully with a red pen. Fill in all the boxes with the same *kana*. Do not scribble. Try to maintain the correct overall shape of the *kana*.

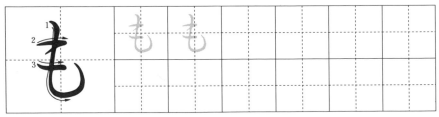

ya

Ya is the "**Ya**!" Germans say when drinking beer from a big mug.

Look at the various forms of this *kana*. Notice what is and is not permissible as variants of the same *kana*.

Recognize and learn the differences and similarities between the two *kana* in each pair.

mi		*se*		*ya*
se	*tsu*	*sa*		

Trace over the model *kana* below carefully with a red pen. Fill in all the boxes with the same *kana*. Do not scribble. Try to maintain the correct overall shape of the *kana*.

yu

Yu is sleepy **you** in the morning when your mirror cracks.

Look at the various forms of this *kana*. Notice what is and is not permissible as variants of the same *kana*.

Recognize and learn the differences and similarities between the two *kana* in each pair.

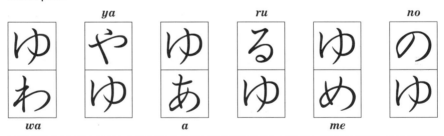

Trace over the model *kana* below carefully with a red pen. Fill in all the boxes with the same *kana*. Do not scribble. Try to maintain the correct overall shape of the *kana*.

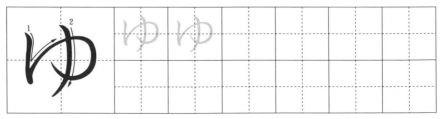

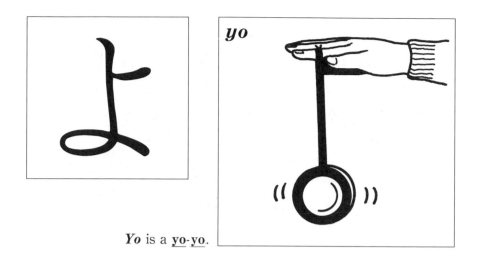

yo

Yo is a **yo-yo**.

Look at the various forms of this *kana*. Notice what is and is not permissible as variants of the same *kana*.

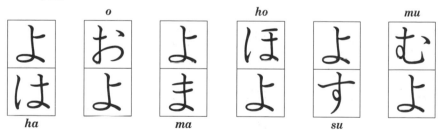

Recognize and learn the differences and similarities between the two *kana* in each pair.

o / *ha*

ho / *ma*

mu / *su*

Trace over the model *kana* below carefully with a red pen. Fill in all the boxes with the same *kana*. Do not scribble. Try to maintain the correct overall shape of the *kana*.

Rah!

Ra is the "**Rah**!" you shout through a megaphone at a game.

Look at the various forms of this *kana*. Notice what is and is not permissible as variants of the same *kana*.

ら　ら　ら　ら　ら　ら

Recognize and learn the differences and similarities between the two *kana* in each pair.

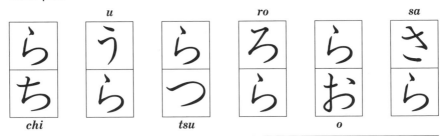

Trace over the model *kana* below carefully with a red pen. Fill in all the boxes with the same *kana*. Do not scribble. Try to maintain the correct overall shape of the *kana*.

54

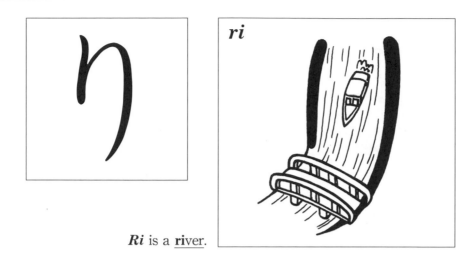

ri

Ri is a **ri**ver.

Look at the various forms of this *kana*. Notice what is and is not permissible as variants of the same *kana*.

Recognize and learn the differences and similarities between the two *kana* in each pair.

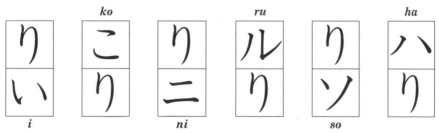

ko *ru* *ha*

i *ni* *so*

Trace over the model *kana* below carefully with a red pen. Fill in all the boxes with the same *kana*. Do not scribble. Try to maintain the correct overall shape of the *kana*.

Ru is a lasso **loo**p.

Look at the various forms of this *kana*. Notice what is and is not permissible as variants of the same *kana*.

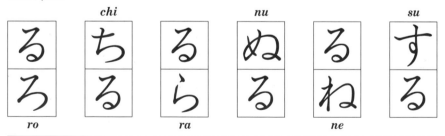

Recognize and learn the differences and similarities between the two *kana* in each pair.

 chi *nu* *su*

ro   *ra*   *ne*

Trace over the model *kana* below carefully with a red pen. Fill in all the boxes with the same *kana*. Do not scribble. Try to maintain the correct overall shape of the *kana*.

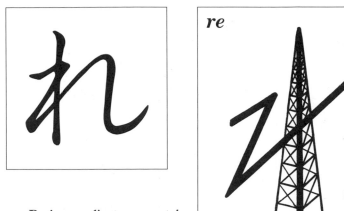

Re is a **ra**<u>dio</u> tower catching **ra**<u>dio</u> waves.

Look at the various forms of this *kana*. Notice what is and is not permissible as variants of the same *kana*.

れ	れ	れ	れ	れ	れ

Recognize and learn the differences and similarities between the two *kana* in each pair.

 ne *n* *yu*

wa *me* *so*

Trace over the model *kana* below carefully with a red pen. Fill in all the boxes with the same *kana*. Do not scribble. Try to maintain the correct overall shape of the *kana*.

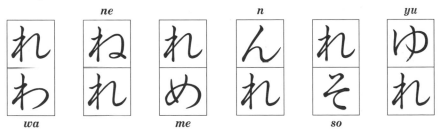

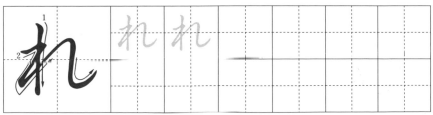

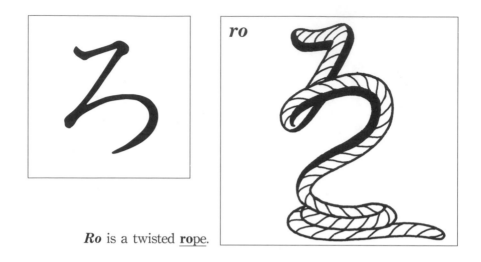

ro

Ro is a twisted **ro**pe.

Look at the various forms of this *kana*. Notice what is and is not permissible as variants of the same *kana*.

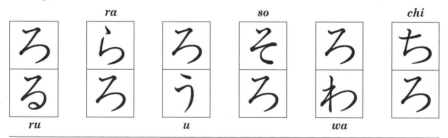

Recognize and learn the differences and similarities between the two *kana* in each pair.

 ra *so* *chi*

ru *u* *wa*

Trace over the model *kana* below carefully with a red pen. Fill in all the boxes with the same *kana*. Do not scribble. Try to maintain the correct overall shape of the *kana*.

wa

Wa is a <u>swa</u>n behind a stake.

Look at the various forms of this *kana*. Notice what is and is not permissible as variants of the same *kana*.

Recognize and learn the differences and similarities between the two *kana* in each pair.

ne   *ra*   *tsu*

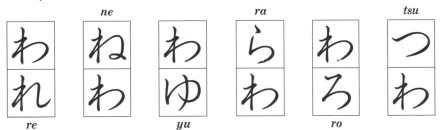

re   *yu*   *ro*

Trace over the model *kana* below carefully with a red pen. Fill in all the boxes with the same *kana*. Do not scribble. Try to maintain the correct overall shape of the *kana*.

O is an **o**l**d** skater skill-
fully skating.

Look at the various forms of this *kana*. Notice what is and is not permissible
as variants of the same *kana*.

を　を　を　を　を　を

Recognize and learn the differences and similarities between the two *kana* in
each pair.

Trace over the model *kana* below carefully with a red pen. Fill in all the boxes
with the same *kana*. Do not scribble. Try to maintain the correct overall shape
of the *kana*.

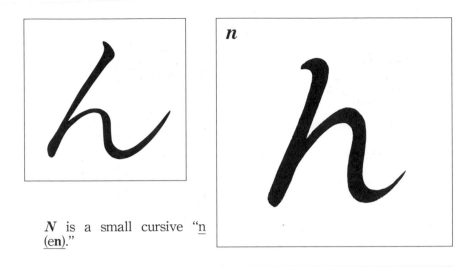

n

N is a small cursive "n
(e**n**)."

Look at the various forms of this *kana*. Notice what is and is not permissible
as variants of the same *kana*.

Recognize and learn the differences and similarities between the two *kana* in
each pair.

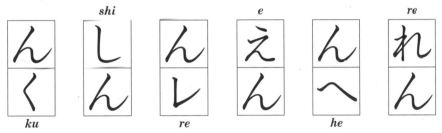

Trace over the model *kana* below carefully with a red pen. Fill in all the boxes
with the same *kana*. Do not scribble. Try to maintain the correct overall shape
of the *kana*.

KATAKANA

Just like *hiragana*, there are 46 basic *katakana* signs. Modified *katakana* signs based on these basic ones represent the remaining syllables. For the explanations of such modifications, see the end of this book.

	a	i	u	e	o
	ア	イ	ウ	エ	オ
k-	カ	キ	ク	ケ	コ
s-	サ	シ	ス	セ	ソ
t-	タ	チ	ツ	テ	ト
n-	ナ	ニ	ヌ	ネ	ノ
h-	ハ	ヒ	フ	ヘ	ホ
m-	マ	ミ	ム	メ	モ
y-	ヤ		ユ		ヨ
r-	ラ	リ	ル	レ	ロ
w-	ワ				ヲ
n	ン				

A is the "**Ahh!**" a hippo shouts.

Look at the various forms of this *kana*. Notice what is and is not permissible as variants of the same *kana*.

Recognize and learn the differences and similarities between the two *kana* in each pair.

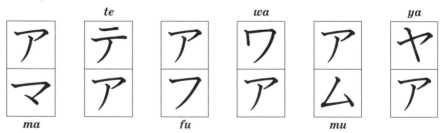

Trace over the model *kana* below carefully with a red pen. Fill in all the boxes with the same *kana*. Do not scribble. Try to maintain the correct overall shape of the *kana*.

64

i

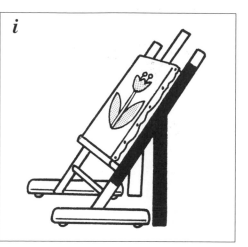

I is an **ea**sel holding a picture.

Look at the various forms of this *kana*. Notice what is and is not permissible as variants of the same *kana*.

Recognize and learn the differences and similarities between the two *kana* in each pair.

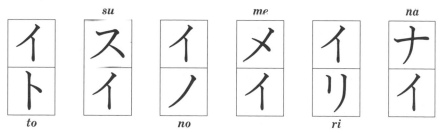

su **me** **na**

to **no** **ri**

Trace over the model *kana* below carefully with a red pen. Fill in all the boxes with the same *kana*. Do not scribble. Try to maintain the correct overall shape of the *kana*.

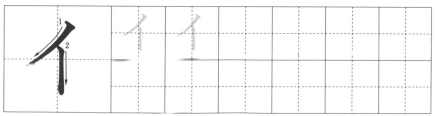

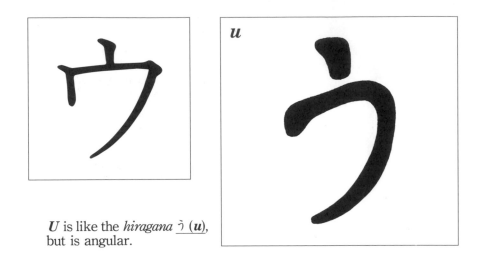

_u_

_U_ is like the _hiragana_ う (_u_), but is angular.

Look at the various forms of this _kana_. Notice what is and is not permissible as variants of the same _kana_.

Recognize and learn the differences and similarities between the two _kana_ in each pair.

_ra_   _ro_   _u_

_wa_   _o_   _fu_

Trace over the model _kana_ below carefully with a red pen. Fill in all the boxes with the same _kana_. Do not scribble. Try to maintain the correct overall shape of the _kana_.

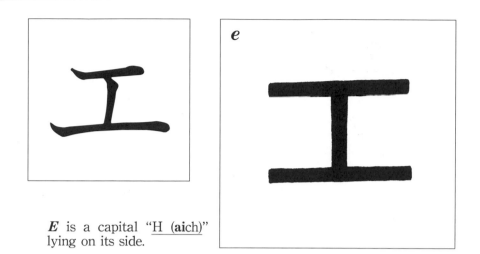

e

_E_ is a capital "H (**ai**ch)" lying on its side.

Look at the various forms of this *kana*. Notice what is and is not permissible as variants of the same *kana*.

Recognize and learn the differences and similarities between the two *kana* in each pair.

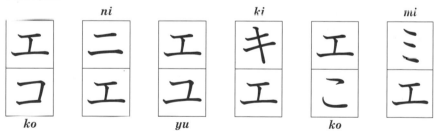

ni   *ki*   *mi*

ko   *yu*   *ko*

Trace over the model *kana* below carefully with a red pen. Fill in all the boxes with the same *kana*. Do not scribble. Try to maintain the correct overall shape of the *kana*.

O is for "**Oh**, what a good dancer!"

Look at the various forms of this *kana*. Notice what is and is not permissible as variants of the same *kana*.

Recognize and learn the differences and similarities between the two *kana* in each pair.

Trace over the model *kana* below carefully with a red pen. Fill in all the boxes with the same *kana*. Do not scribble. Try to maintain the correct overall shape of the *kana*.

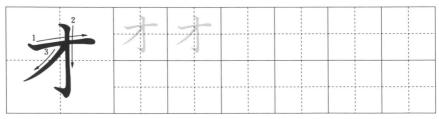

ka

Ka is an angular *hiragana* か(**ka**) without the crow.

Look at the various forms of this *kana*. Notice what is and is not permissible as variants of the same *kana*.

Recognize and learn the differences and similarities between the two *kana* in each pair.

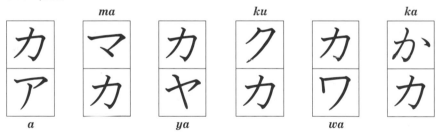

	ma		*ku*		*ka*
カ	マ	カ	ク	カ	か
ア	カ	ヤ	カ	ワ	カ
a		*ya*		*wa*	

Trace over the model *kana* below carefully with a red pen. Fill in all the boxes with the same *kana*. Do not scribble. Try to maintain the correct overall shape of the *kana*.

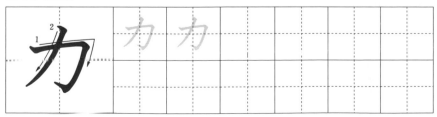

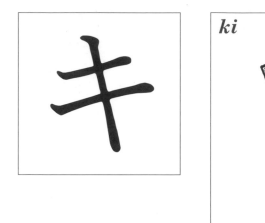

ki

Ki is a <u>key</u> without a loop.

Look at the various forms of this *kana*. Notice what is and is not permissible as variants of the same *kana*.

Recognize and learn the differences and similarities between the two *kana* in each pair.

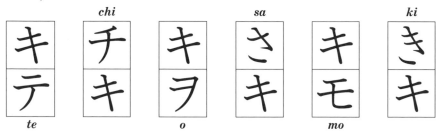

chi		*sa*		*ki*
te		*o*		*mo*

Trace over the model *kana* below carefully with a red pen. Fill in all the boxes with the same *kana*. Do not scribble. Try to maintain the correct overall shape of the *kana*.

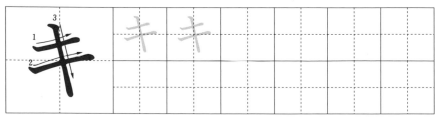

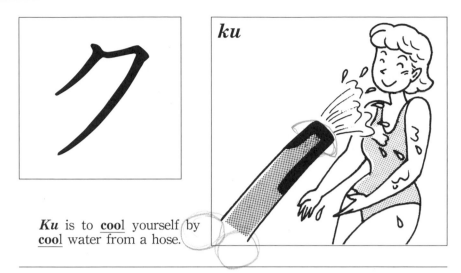

ku

Ku is to **coo**l yourself by **coo**l water from a hose.

Look at the various forms of this *kana*. Notice what is and is not permissible as variants of the same *kana*.

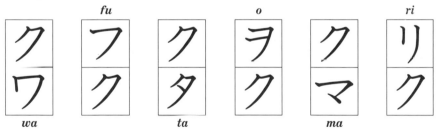

Recognize and learn the differences and similarities between the two *kana* in each pair.

fu		*o*		*ri*

wa		*ta*		*ma*

Trace over the model *kana* below carefully with a red pen. Fill in all the boxes with the same *kana*. Do not scribble. Try to maintain the correct overall shape of the *kana*.

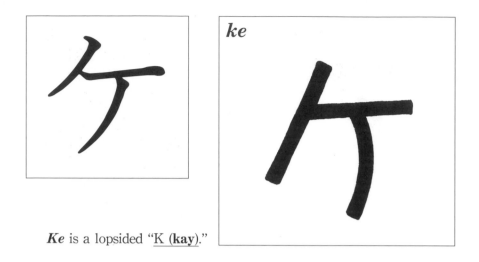

ke

Ke is a lopsided "K (**kay**)."

Look at the various forms of this *kana*. Notice what is and is not permissible as variants of the same *kana*.

Recognize and learn the differences and similarities between the two *kana* in each pair.

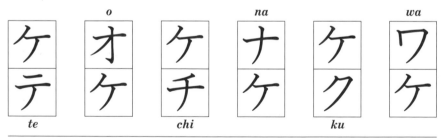

Trace over the model *kana* below carefully with a red pen. Fill in all the boxes with the same *kana*. Do not scribble. Try to maintain the correct overall shape of the *kana*.

72

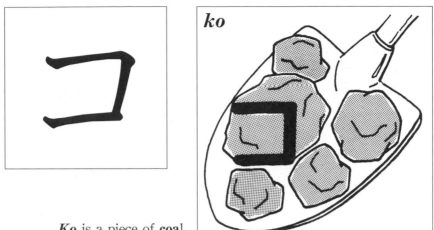

ko

Ko is a piece of **coa**l.

Look at the various forms of this *kana*. Notice what is and is not permissible as variants of the same *kana*.

Recognize and learn the differences and similarities between the two *kana* in each pair.

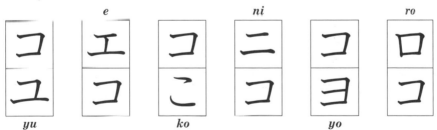

Trace over the model *kana* below carefully with a red pen. Fill in all the boxes with the same *kana*. Do not scribble. Try to maintain the correct overall shape of the *kana*.

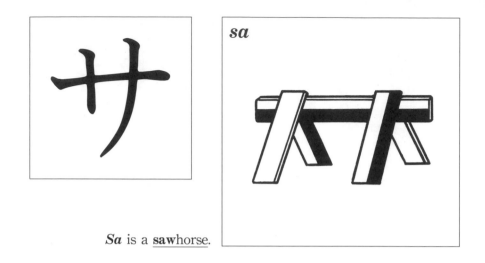

sa

Sa is a **saw**horse.

Look at the various forms of this *kana*. Notice what is and is not permissible as variants of the same *kana*.

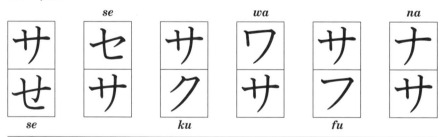

Recognize and learn the differences and similarities between the two *kana* in each pair.

 se *wa* *na*

se   *ku*   *fu*

Trace over the model *kana* below carefully with a red pen. Fill in all the boxes with the same *kana*. Do not scribble. Try to maintain the correct overall shape of the *kana*.

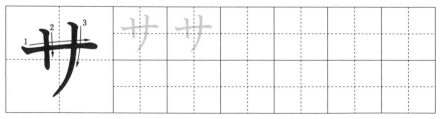

shi

Shi is for "**She** has good-looking lips and jaws."

Look at the various forms of this *kana*. Notice what is and is not permissible as variants of the same *kana*.

Recognize and learn the differences and similarities between the two *kana* in each pair.

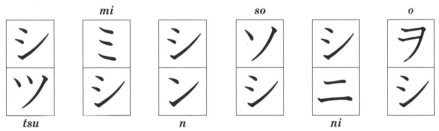

	mi		*so*		*o*
tsu		*n*		*ni*	

Trace over the model *kana* below carefully with a red pen. Fill in all the boxes with the same *kana*. Do not scribble. Try to maintain the correct overall shape of the *kana*.

Su is **Su**perman.

Look at the various forms of this *kana*. Notice what is and is not permissible as variants of the same *kana*.

Recognize and learn the differences and similarities between the two *kana* in each pair.

ma
me
ta
fu
nu
ke

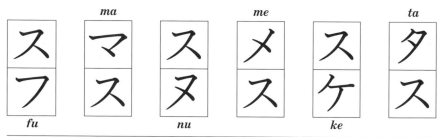

Trace over the model *kana* below carefully with a red pen. Fill in all the boxes with the same *kana*. Do not scribble. Try to maintain the correct overall shape of the *kana*.

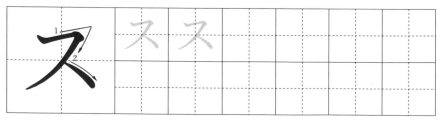

se

Se is to **say** "I love you too!"

Look at the various forms of this *kana*. Notice what is and is not permissible as variants of the same *kana*.

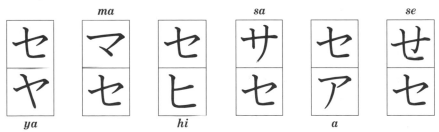

Recognize and learn the differences and similarities between the two *kana* in each pair.

ma

sa

se

ya

hi

a

Trace over the model *kana* below carefully with a red pen. Fill in all the boxes with the same *kana*. Do not scribble. Try to maintain the correct overall shape of the *kana*.

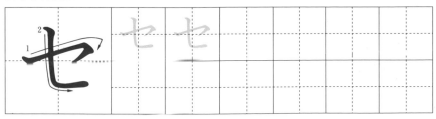

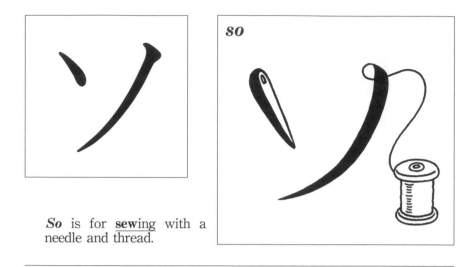

_So_ is for **sew**ing with a needle and thread.

Look at the various forms of this _kana_. Notice what is and is not permissible as variants of the same _kana_.

Recognize and learn the differences and similarities between the two _kana_ in each pair.

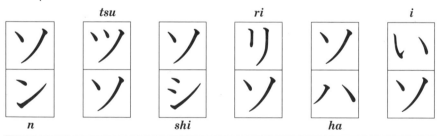

Trace over the model _kana_ below carefully with a red pen. Fill in all the boxes with the same _kana_. Do not scribble. Try to maintain the correct overall shape of the _kana_.

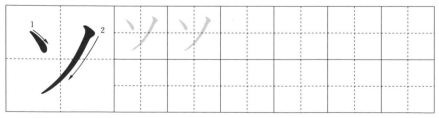

78

Ta is the Leaning **To**wer of Pisa.

Look at the various forms of this *kana*. Notice what is and is not permissible as variants of the same *kana*.

タ タ タ タ タ ワ

Recognize and learn the differences and similarities between the two *kana* in each pair.

wa *ma* *mo*

ku *nu* *o*

Trace over the model *kana* below carefully with a red pen. Fill in all the boxes with the same *kana*. Do not scribble. Try to maintain the correct overall shape of the *kana*.

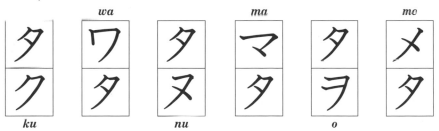

chi

Chi is a **chee**rleader.

Look at the various forms of this *kana*. Notice what is and is not permissible as variants of the same *kana*.

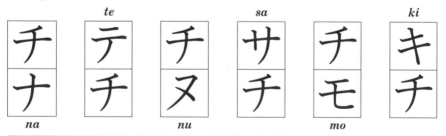

Recognize and learn the differences and similarities between the two *kana* in each pair.

Trace over the model *kana* below carefully with a red pen. Fill in all the boxes with the same *kana*. Do not scribble. Try to maintain the correct overall shape of the *kana*.

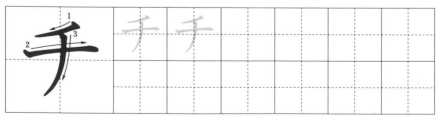

80

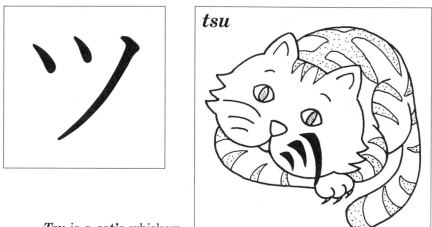

tsu

Tsu is a <u>cat's</u> whiskers.

Look at the various forms of this *kana*. Notice what is and is not permissible as variants of the same *kana*.

Recognize and learn the differences and similarities between the two *kana* in each pair.

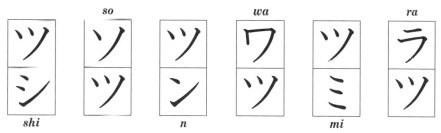

Trace over the model *kana* below carefully with a red pen. Fill in all the boxes with the same *kana*. Do not scribble. Try to maintain the correct overall shape of the *kana*.

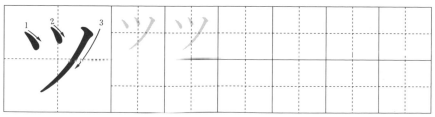

Te is a **ta**ble.

Look at the various forms of this *kana*. Notice what is and is not permissible as variants of the same *kana*.

Recognize and learn the differences and similarities between the two *kana* in each pair.

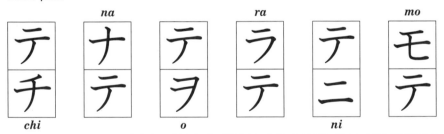

Trace over the model *kana* below carefully with a red pen. Fill in all the boxes with the same *kana*. Do not scribble. Try to maintain the correct overall shape of the *kana*.

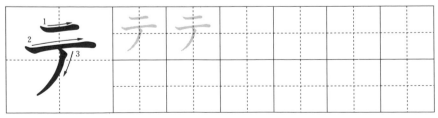

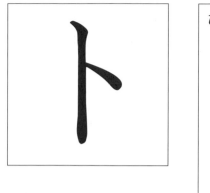

to

To is the right side of a **to**tem pole.

Look at the various forms of this *kana*. Notice what is and is not permissible as variants of the same *kana*.

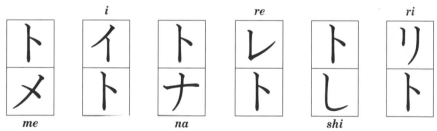

Recognize and learn the differences and similarities between the two *kana* in each pair.

	i		*re*		*ri*

me   *na*   *shi*

Trace over the model *kana* below carefully with a red pen. Fill in all the boxes with the same *kana*. Do not scribble. Try to maintain the correct overall shape of the *kana*.

Na is a door without a **kno**cker.

Look at the various forms of this *kana*. Notice what is and is not permissible as variants of the same *kana*.

ナ	ナ	ナ	ナ	ナ	ナ

Recognize and learn the differences and similarities between the two *kana* in each pair.

Trace over the model *kana* below carefully with a red pen. Fill in all the boxes with the same *kana*. Do not scribble. Try to maintain the correct overall shape of the *kana*.

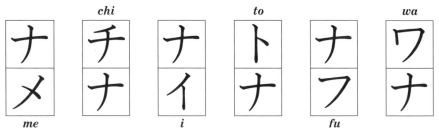

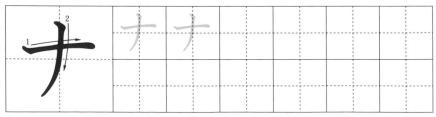

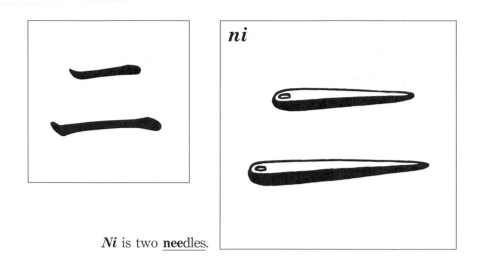

ni

Ni is two **nee**dles.

Look at the various forms of this *kana*. Notice what is and is not permissible as variants of the same *kana*.

Recognize and learn the differences and similarities between the two *kana* in each pair.

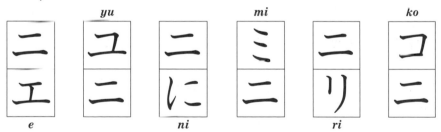

yu	mi	ko
e	ni	ri

Trace over the model *kana* below carefully with a red pen. Fill in all the boxes with the same *kana*. Do not scribble. Try to maintain the correct overall shape of the *kana*.

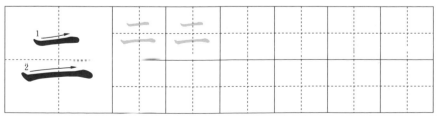

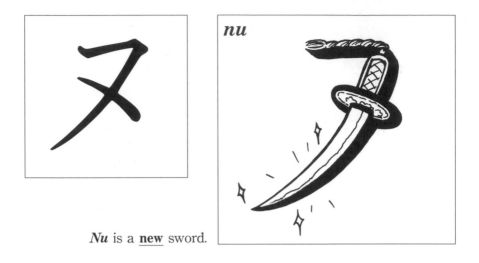

Nu is a **new** sword.

Look at the various forms of this *kana*. Notice what is and is not permissible as variants of the same *kana*.

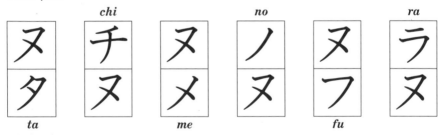

Recognize and learn the differences and similarities between the two *kana* in each pair.

	chi		*no*		*ra*

| *ta* | | *me* | | *fu* | |

Trace over the model *kana* below carefully with a red pen. Fill in all the boxes with the same *kana*. Do not scribble. Try to maintain the correct overall shape of the *kana*.

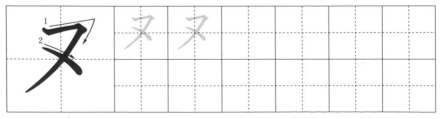

86

ne

Ne is a bird's **ne**st in a tree.

Look at the various forms of this *kana*. Notice what is and is not permissible as variants of the same *kana*.

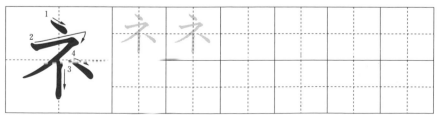

Recognize and learn the differences and similarities between the two *kana* in each pair.

e　　*o*　　*nu*

su　　*ho*　　*ya*

Trace over the model *kana* below carefully with a red pen. Fill in all the boxes with the same *kana*. Do not scribble. Try to maintain the correct overall shape of the *kana*.

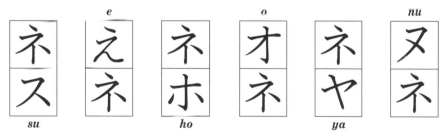

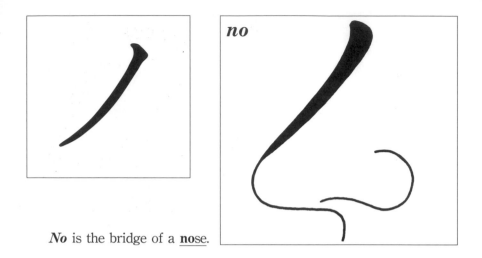

no

No is the bridge of a **no**se.

Look at the various forms of this *kana*. Notice what is and is not permissible as variants of the same *kana*.

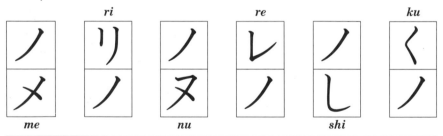

Recognize and learn the differences and similarities between the two *kana* in each pair.

	ri		*re*		*ku*

me   *nu*   *shi*

Trace over the model *kana* below carefully with a red pen. Fill in all the boxes with the same *kana*. Do not scribble. Try to maintain the correct overall shape of the *kana*.

88

ha

Ha is a **haw**k laughing
"**Ha-ha!**"

Look at the various forms of this *kana*. Notice what is and is not permissible as variants of the same *kana*.

Recognize and learn the differences and similarities between the two *kana* in each pair.

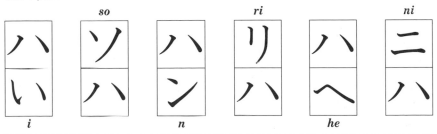

Trace over the model *kana* below carefully with a red pen. Fill in all the boxes with the same *kana*. Do not scribble. Try to maintain the correct overall shape of the *kana*.

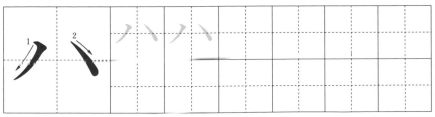

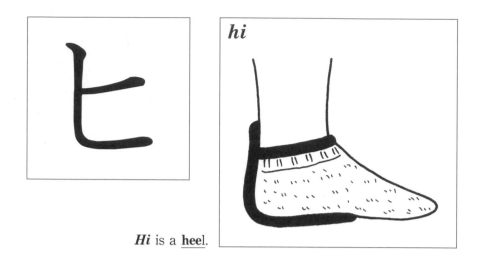

Hi is a <u>hee</u>l.

Look at the various forms of this *kana*. Notice what is and is not permissible as variants of the same *kana*.

Recognize and learn the differences and similarities between the two *kana* in each pair.

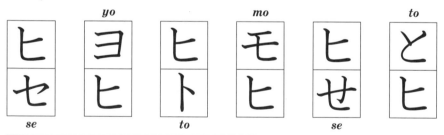

Trace over the model *kana* below carefully with a red pen. Fill in all the boxes with the same *kana*. Do not scribble. Try to maintain the correct overall shape of the *kana*.

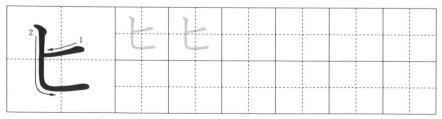

90

fu/hu

Fu/Hu is Little Red Riding **Hood**.

Look at the various forms of this *kana*. Notice what is and is not permissible as variants of the same *kana*.

フ　フ　フ　フ　フ　ワ

Recognize and learn the differences and similarities between the two *kana* in each pair.

Trace over the model *kana* below carefully with a red pen. Fill in all the boxes with the same *kana*. Do not scribble. Try to maintain the correct overall shape of the *kana*.

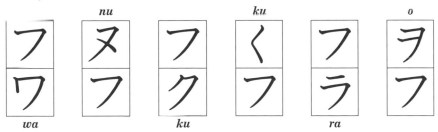

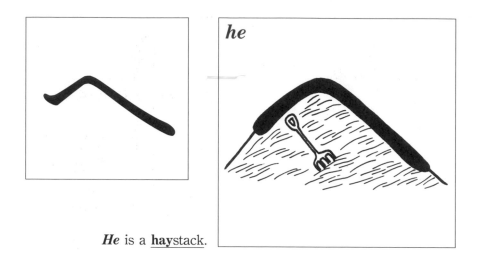

He is a **hay**stack.

Look at the various forms of this *kana*. Notice what is and is not permissible as variants of the same *kana*.

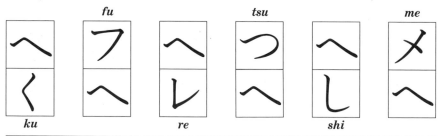

Recognize and learn the differences and similarities between the two *kana* in each pair.

Trace over the model *kana* below carefully with a red pen. Fill in all the boxes with the same *kana*. Do not scribble. Try to maintain the correct overall shape of the *kana*.

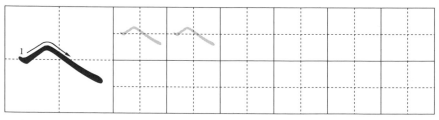

ho

Ho is a **ho**ly cross with two people at prayer.

Look at the various forms of this *kana*. Notice what is and is not permissible as variants of the same *kana*.

Recognize and learn the differences and similarities between the two *kana* in each pair.

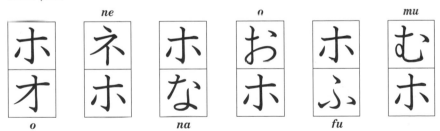

Trace over the model *kana* below carefully with a red pen. Fill in all the boxes with the same *kana*. Do not scribble. Try to maintain the correct overall shape of the *kana*.

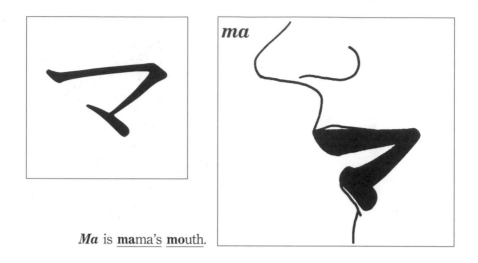

ma

Ma is **ma**ma's **mouth**.

Look at the various forms of this *kana*. Notice what is and is not permissible as variants of the same *kana*.

Recognize and learn the differences and similarities between the two *kana* in each pair.

mu   *se*   *tsu*

a   *ya*   *nu*

Trace over the model *kana* below carefully with a red pen. Fill in all the boxes with the same *kana*. Do not scribble. Try to maintain the correct overall shape of the *kana*.

94

mi

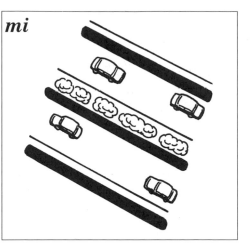

Mi is the <u>me</u>dian strip of a highway.

Look at the various forms of this *kana*. Notice what is and is not permissible as variants of the same *kana*.

Recognize and learn the differences and similarities between the two *kana* in each pair.

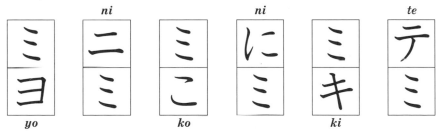

Trace over the model *kana* below carefully with a red pen. Fill in all the boxes with the same *kana*. Do not scribble. Try to maintain the correct overall shape of the *kana*.

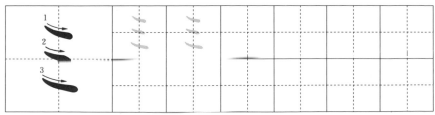

mu

Mu is a **moo**se with huge antlers.

Look at the various forms of this *kana*. Notice what is and is not permissible as variants of the same *kana*.

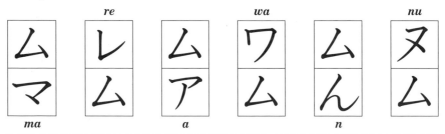

Recognize and learn the differences and similarities between the two *kana* in each pair.

re

ma

wa

a

nu

n

Trace over the model *kana* below carefully with a red pen. Fill in all the boxes with the same *kana*. Do not scribble. Try to maintain the correct overall shape of the *kana*.

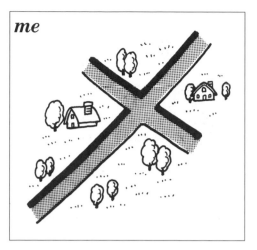

me

Me is two roads that have **me**t.

Look at the various forms of this *kana*. Notice what is and is not permissible as variants of the same *kana*.

Recognize and learn the differences and similarities between the two *kana* in each pair.

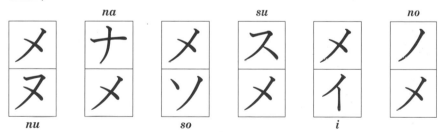

	na		*su*		*no*
メ	ナ	メ	ス	メ	ノ
ヌ	メ	ソ	メ	イ	メ
nu		*so*		*i*	

Trace over the model *kana* below carefully with a red pen. Fill in all the boxes with the same *kana*. Do not scribble. Try to maintain the correct overall shape of the *kana*.

97

Mo is for **mow**ing grass with a handleless sickle.

Look at the various forms of this *kana*. Notice what is and is not permissible as variants of the same *kana*.

モ	モ	モ	モ	モ	モ

Recognize and learn the differences and similarities between the two *kana* in each pair.

Trace over the model *kana* below carefully with a red pen. Fill in all the boxes with the same *kana*. Do not scribble. Try to maintain the correct overall shape of the *kana*.

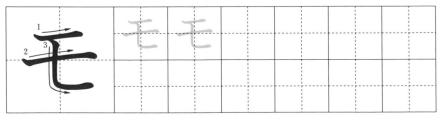

ya

Ya is the "**Ya**!" Germans say after finishing their beer.

Look at the various forms of this *kana*. Notice what is and is not permissible as variants of the same *kana*.

ヤ ヤ ヤ ヤ ヤ ヤ

Recognize and learn the differences and similarities between the two *kana* in each pair.

a		*se*		*ya*
ヤ	ア	ヤ	セ	ヤ	や
マ	ヤ	カ	ヤ	セ	ヤ
ma		*ka*		*se*

Trace over the model *kana* below carefully with a red pen. Fill in all the boxes with the same *kana*. Do not scribble. Try to maintain the correct overall shape of the *kana*.

yu

Yu is a **U-HAUL** van.

Look at the various forms of this *kana*. Notice what is and is not permissible as variants of the same *kana*.

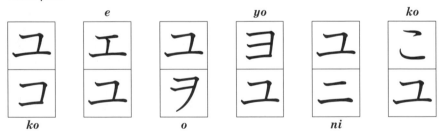

Recognize and learn the differences and similarities between the two *kana* in each pair.

ko

e

o

yo

ni

ko

Trace over the model *kana* below carefully with a red pen. Fill in all the boxes with the same *kana*. Do not scribble. Try to maintain the correct overall shape of the *kana*.

100

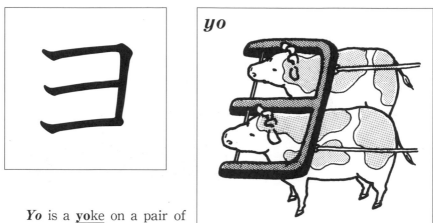

yo

_Yo_ is a **yo**ke on a pair of oxen.

Look at the various forms of this *kana*. Notice what is and is not permissible as variants of the same *kana*.

Recognize and learn the differences and similarities between the two *kana* in each pair.

Trace over the model *kana* below carefully with a red pen. Fill in all the boxes with the same *kana*. Do not scribble. Try to maintain the correct overall shape of the *kana*.

101

_Ra_ is a **ro**cking chair.

Look at the various forms of this _kana_. Notice what is and is not permissible as variants of the same _kana_.

Recognize and learn the differences and similarities between the two _kana_ in each pair.

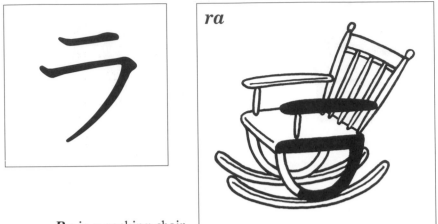

Trace over the model _kana_ below carefully with a red pen. Fill in all the boxes with the same _kana_. Do not scribble. Try to maintain the correct overall shape of the _kana_.

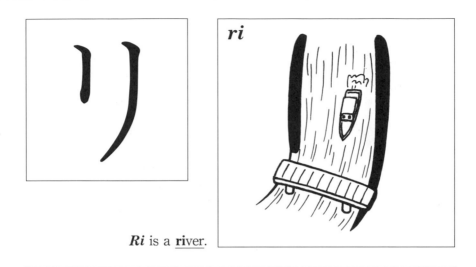

ri

Ri is a <u>ri</u>ver.

Look at the various forms of this *kana*. Notice what is and is not permissible as variants of the same *kana*.

Recognize and learn the differences and similarities between the two *kana* in each pair.

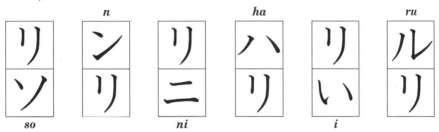

Trace over the model *kana* below carefully with a red pen. Fill in all the boxes with the same *kana*. Do not scribble. Try to maintain the correct overall shape of the *kana*.

103

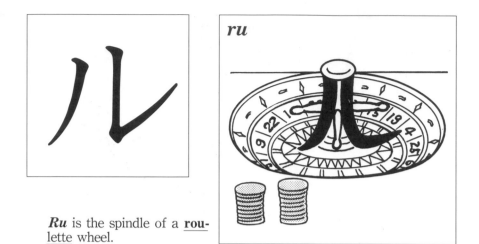

ru

Ru is the spindle of a **rou-**
lette wheel.

Look at the various forms of this *kana*. Notice what is and is not permissible as variants of the same *kana*.

Recognize and learn the differences and similarities between the two *kana* in each pair.

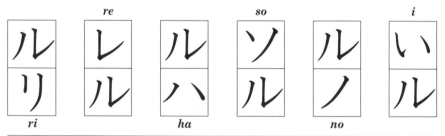

re
so
i
ri
ha
no

Trace over the model *kana* below carefully with a red pen. Fill in all the boxes with the same *kana*. Do not scribble. Try to maintain the correct overall shape of the *kana*.

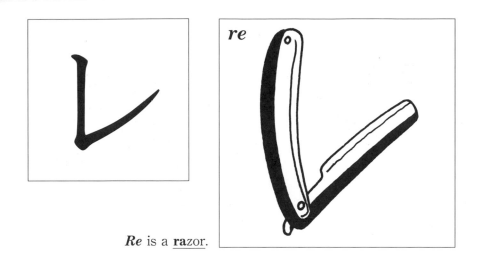

Re is a **ra**zor.

Look at the various forms of this *kana*. Notice what is and is not permissible as variants of the same *kana*.

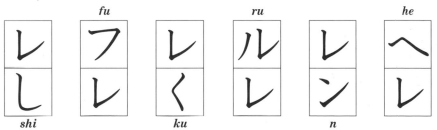

Recognize and learn the differences and similarities between the two *kana* in each pair.

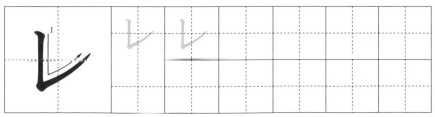

Trace over the model *kana* below carefully with a red pen. Fill in all the boxes with the same *kana*. Do not scribble. Try to maintain the correct overall shape of the *kana*.

105

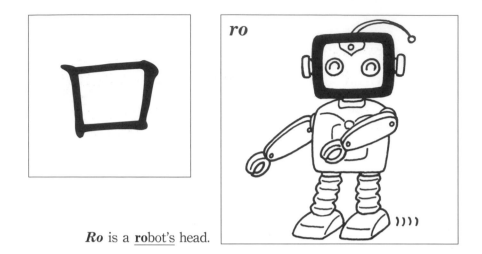

ro

Ro is a **ro**bot's head.

Look at the various forms of this *kana*. Notice what is and is not permissible as variants of the same *kana*.

Recognize and learn the differences and similarities between the two *kana* in each pair.

yu   *i*   *ni*

ko   *ni*   *yo*

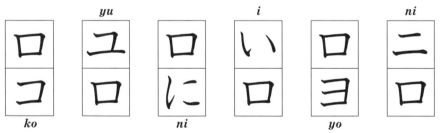

Trace over the model *kana* below carefully with a red pen. Fill in all the boxes with the same *kana*. Do not scribble. Try to maintain the correct overall shape of the *kana*.

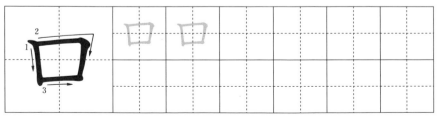

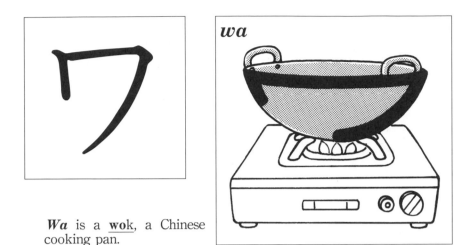

Wa is a **wo**k, a Chinese cooking pan.

Look at the various forms of this *kana*. Notice what is and is not permissible as variants of the same *kana*.

Recognize and learn the differences and similarities between the two *kana* in each pair.

fu

ya

u

ku

ra

ka

Trace over the model *kana* below carefully with a red pen. Fill in all the boxes with the same *kana*. Do not scribble. Try to maintain the correct overall shape of the *kana*.

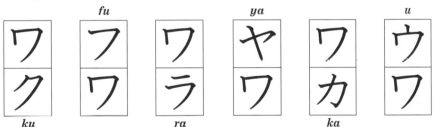

O is an <u>o</u>cean liner.

Look at the various forms of this *kana*. Notice what is and is not permissible as variants of the same *kana*.

Recognize and learn the differences and similarities between the two *kana* in each pair.

Trace over the model *kana* below carefully with a red pen. Fill in all the boxes with the same *kana*. Do not scribble. Try to maintain the correct overall shape of the *kana*.

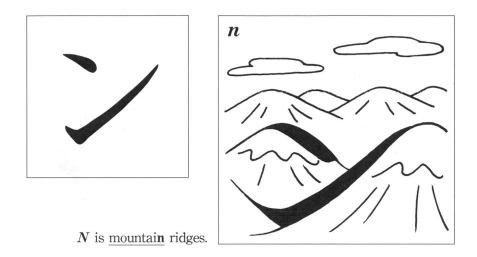

n

N is <u>mountain</u> ridges.

Look at the various forms of this *kana*. Notice what is and is not permissible as variants of the same *kana*.

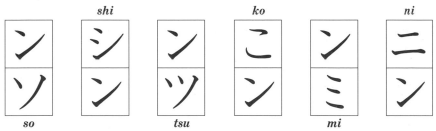

Recognize and learn the differences and similarities between the two *kana* in each pair.

 shi *ko*   *ni*

so *tsu* *mi*

Trace over the model *kana* below carefully with a red pen. Fill in all the boxes with the same *kana*. Do not scribble. Try to maintain the correct overall shape of the *kana*.

APPENDIX

I. ELABORATIONS OF BASIC
    HIRAGANA AND *KATAKANA*

II. PUNCTUATION MARKS

I. ELABORATIONS OF BASIC *HIRAGANA* AND *KATAKANA*

1. *HIRAGANA*

In addition to the basic 46 *hiragana* representing 46 syllables, there are many more signs needed for the other syllables in Japanese. All the other syllables can be represented by slight elaborations of basic *hiragana*.

1. 1. *Hiragana* with two dots

The four lines of syllables with voiced consonants (for example, English g, z, d and b) are represented by adding two dots at the upper right-hand corner of the corresponding *hiragana*. Due to historical circumstances, *ba-bi-bu-be-bo* syllables are related to *ha-hi-hu-he-ho*.

	a	*i*	*u*	*e*	*o*
g-	が	ぎ	ぐ	げ	ご
z-	ざ	じ	ず	ぜ	ぞ
d-	だ	ぢ	づ	で	ど
b-	ば	び	ぶ	べ	ぼ

In most cases, じ and ず are used for *ji* and *zu* respectively instead of ぢ and づ. In compounds, the initial syllable of the second word quite commonly receives two dots (or voicing) if the initial syllable is of basic *hiragana*. For example, if such initial syllables are either ち *chi* or つ *tsu*, they become ぢ *ji* or づ *zu* respectively in compounds, as follows:

はな *hana* + ち *chi* → はなぢ *hanaji*
(nose)   (blood)   (nosebleeding)

みか *mika* + つき *tsuki* → みかづき *mikazuki*
(three days) (moon)   (crescent moon)

Also, after *chi* and *tsu*, ぢ *ji* and づ *zu* tend to be used instead of じ *ji* and ず *zu* respectively.

ちぢむ *chijimu*   つづく *tsuzuku*
(to shrink)   (to continue)

112

1. 2. *Hiragana* with a little circle

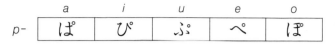

	a	i	u	e	o
p-	ぱ	ぴ	ぷ	ぺ	ぽ

Pa-pi-pu-pe-po syllables are related to *ha-hi-hu-he-ho* for historical reasons and represented by adding a little circle at the upper right-hand corner of *hiragana* for *ha-hi-hu-he-ho* syllables.

1. 3. Small や (*ya*), ゆ (*yu*), よ (*yo*)

	a	u	o
ky-	きゃ	きゅ	きょ
sh-	しゃ	しゅ	しょ
ch-	ちゃ	ちゅ	ちょ
ny-	にゃ	にゅ	にょ
hy-	ひゃ	ひゅ	ひょ
my-	みゃ	みゅ	みょ
ry-	りゃ	りゅ	りょ
gy	ぎゃ	ぎゅ	ぎょ
j-	じゃ	じゅ	じょ
by-	びゃ	びゅ	びょ
py-	ぴゃ	ぴゅ	ぴょ

Syllables containing a short "y" sound such as *kya*, *hyo*, or even *shu* (*syu*) are represented by the combination of basic *hiragana* of the *i* column such as *ki*, *shi*, and *hi*, and small-sized *ya*, *yu*, and *yo*. These small *ya*, *yu* and *yo* are placed in the lower half of a line if they are written horizontally.

If they are written vertically, which is possible in Japanese, they are placed to the right of a column:

きゃ *kya*   みゅ *myu*   ぴょ *pyo*

1. 4. Long vowels

There are long vowels such as ā, ī, ū, ē, and ō in Japanese.

The *a* column

Long vowels such as ā, kā, sā, and tā, i.e., those of the *a* column, are represented by adding あ (*a*) to the first syllables:

あ あ *ā*   か あ *kā*   さ あ *sā*

The *i* column

Long vowels such as ī, kī, chī, and mī, i.e., those of the *i* column, are represented by adding い (*i*) to the first syllables:

い い *ī*   き い *kī*   み い *mī*

The *u* column

Long vowels such as ū, sū, yū, i.e., those of the *u* column, are represented by adding う (*u*) to the first syllables:

う う *ū*   す う *sū*   ゆ う *yū*

The *e* column

Long vowels such as rē, kē, sē, tē, i.e., those of the *e* column, are usually represented by adding い (*i*) [not え (*e*)!] to the first syllables:

れ い *rē*   け い *kē*   せ い *sē*

But there are exceptions like the following:

え え *ē*   ね え *nē*   お ね え さ ん   *onēsan*
(yes)   (I say)   (an elder sister)

The *o* column

Long vowels of the *o* column such as ō, kō, sō, and tō are represented by adding う (*u*) [not お (*o*)!] to the first syllables:

お う *ō*   こ う *kō*   そ う *sō*

But there are some exceptions:

お お き *Ōki*   お お き い *ōkii*   と お い *tōi*
[family name]   (big)   (far)

お お い *ōi*   と お り *tōri*   と お る *tōru*
(numerous)   (street)   (to pass)

こ お る *kōru*
(to freeze)

1. 5. Little つ (*tsu*)

When two consonants except for *n* are in a row, the first consonant is represented by a little つ (*tsu*) written in the lower half of a horizontal line or to the right of a vertical column:

いっぱい *ippai*   みっつ *mittsu*   か
                                              っ *katta*
                                              た

1. 6. Particles *wa*, *e* and *o*

The three particles (grammatical markers) in Japanese, *wa* (a particle of topic), *e* (a particle of direction), and *o* (a particle of direct object), are conventionally represented by は (*ha*), へ (*he*) and を (*o*), respectively, due to historical circumstances. は, へ and を are pronounced as *wa*, *e* and *o*, respectively.

わたし は これ を よむ。 *Watashi wa kore o yomu.*

とうきょう へ いく。 *Tōkyō e iku.*

2. *KATAKANA*

Most of the modifications applied to *hiragana* can also be applied to *katakana*. Notice one difference between *hiragana* and *katakana* with respect to long vowels.

2. 1. *Katakana* with two dots

The same as *hiragana*:

	a	i	u	e	o
g-	ガ	ギ	グ	ゲ	ゴ
z-	ザ	ジ	ズ	ゼ	ゾ
d-	ダ	(ヂ)	(ヅ)	デ	ド
b-	バ	ビ	ブ	ベ	ボ

2. 2. *Katakana* with a little circle

The same as *hiragana*:

	a	i	u	e	o
p-	パ	ピ	プ	ペ	ポ

2. 3. Small ヤ *(ya)*, ユ *(yu)*, ヨ *(yo)*

The same as *hiragana*:

	a	u	o
ky-	キャ	キュ	キョ
sh-	シャ	シュ	ショ
ch-	チャ	チュ	チョ
ny-	ニャ	ニュ	ニョ
hy-	ヒャ	ヒュ	ヒョ
my-	ミャ	ミュ	ミョ
ry-	リャ	リュ	リョ
gy-	ギャ	ギュ	ギョ
j-	ジャ	ジュ	ジョ
by-	ビャ	ビュ	ビョ
py-	ピャ	ピュ	ピョ

2. 4. Long vowels

Long vowels are represented uniformly by drawing a bar in writing *katakana*. A horizontal bar is drawn when written horizontally and a vertical bar is used when written vertically:

アー $\bar{a}$ キー $k\bar{i}$ スー $s\bar{u}$ テー $t\bar{e}$ ノ| $n\bar{o}$

2. 5. Little ッ *(tsu)*

The same as *hiragana*:

コップ *koppu*   ベッド *beddo*

2. 6. Particles *wa, e* and *o*

Since *katakana* are ordinarily reserved for words of foreign origin, Japanese words like grammatical particles are not expressed by *katakana* in ordinary writing. But if special situations necessitate writing all in *katakana*, then these particles are represented just as in *hiragana*:

ワタシ ハ コレ ヲ ヨム。　*Watashi wa kore o yomu.*

トーキョー ヘ イク。　*Tōkyō e iku.*

II. PUNCTUATION MARKS

1. The small circle

The end of a sentence is marked by a small circle in Japanese. When written horizontally, the small circle is placed at the bottom of a line. When written vertically, the small circle is placed to the right of a column.

わたしはいきます。　*Watashi wa ikimasu.*

これはほんです。　*Kore wa hon desu.*

2. The comma

A comma is used to indicate a pause. The position of the comma is the same as the small circle.

はい、そうです。　*Hai, sō desu.*

3. Quotation marks

Quotations are indicated by a pair of signs like corners. When written horizontally, the opening sign is placed in the upper half and the closing sign is placed in the lower half, as follows:

「わたしはたなかです。」といいました。
"Watashi wa Tanaka desu." to iimashita.

When written vertically, the opening sign is placed to the right of a column and the closing sign is placed to the left of the column:

「わたしはたなかです。」といいました。

"Watashi wa Tanaka desu." to iimashita.